IRISH NAMES FOR CHILDREN

PEG COGHLAN

MERCIER PRESS

IRISH AMERICAN BOOK COMPANY (IABC)
Boulder, Colorado

CONTENTS

INTRODUCTION

The names given to children in Ireland, as in all countries in the western world, are affected by four main considerations: family, religion, country and fashion. The first is the strongest and the cause of the persistence of 'older' names. John, Mary, Michael and Anne hold their places because of the risk of offending grandparents, and with these there is the consolation of knowing that the given name works with the surname. The child has little say or recourse except deed poll and I have often wondered what alternate generations of eldest sons made of a family tradition I know of, by which they were named in order Kyril and Methodius, after the ninth-century brother saints from eastern Europe.

Religion as a determinant of Christian names is still strong. Up to quite recently some baptising Catholic priests balked such inventions as 'Kerry' or 'Derry' and insisted on saints' names, however obscure. Fortunately Ireland had more saints than scholars and there was no lack of choice. The many Brigids, Itas, Brendans and Patricks are an indication of initiative on the part of their parents in combining faith with patriotism but there are also lots of Boscos, Pascals, Imeldas and Gorettis to mark personal devotion.

National considerations produced a crop of Patrick Sarsfields, Emmets and Pearses on one side and the occasional Craig and Carson on the other but their frequency is slight compared with the rush of Piuses, Pacellis, Pauls and John Pauls, names that mark consistories. As to names dictated by fashion (of which new popes form a sub-class) they seldom last for long, as the Thedas, Marlenes and Bettes of the 1930s and the Marilyns, Ringos, Jasons and Kylies of more recent times can testify.

The most notable change in the naming of Irish babies has been the recovery of old names from Celtic mythology and of saints' names from that grey-green area of wonders attached to historical personalities. The Letitias, Statias and Minnies of the last century now seem in total eclipse while the Deirdres, Ronans, Niamhs,

Conalls and Caoilfhionns hold their heads high in euphonious patriotism.

This book gives a selection of popular Irish names, with some account of their meanings and histories. Some are millennia old, many came as foreigners and became more Irish than the Irish themselves, and some of permanent international popularity had Irish thrust upon them.

Note

The usual form of the name is followed by its Gaelic equivalent if it is different.

NAMES FOR BOYS

ÁENGUS (ÓENGUS)

[Also Aongus and Aonghus] The Irish equivalent of the popular Scots name Angus, though that spelling is also found in Ireland. The name could mean 'one choice' or 'sole vigour'. In Celtic mythology he was the god of love, the son of Dagda (the Irish Zeus) and Boann, after whom the river Boyne was named. He is usually pictured with four birds circling his head, representing his kisses. The name was borne by several Irish heroes and by saints, notably Óengus the Culdee.

AIDAN (AODHÁN)

[Also Áedán] A diminutive of Aodh and meaning 'little flame'. It was the name of several Irish saints, most famously Aidan of Lindisfarne. After serving as a monk in Iona he was sent to help convert the heathen Anglo-Saxons in Northumbria. He established his monastery on the tidal island of Lindisfarne and made it the centre for the evangelisation of the northern part of England. He died in 651. One interesting result is that the name is not uncommon in England.

AILBE

[Also Ailbhe] This name, which was given to boys and girls, may mean 'white'. Saint Ailbe of Emly (d. 527), who was consecrated bishop in Rome, was a near-contemporary of Saint Patrick, and played an important part in Christianising the south of Ireland. He was known as the Patrick of the south or 'the other Saint Patrick'. The name is sometimes given in English as Alby and is used as the Irish form of Albert, without much authority.

AINDRIAS

[Also Andriú] The Irish form of the biblical Andrew which meant 'manly' in the original Greek.

ALASTAR

Though more common in the Scots vocative form Alastair this Irish name is the equivalent of Alexander (Greek: 'defender of man').

ANTOINE (ANTAINE)

The Gaelicised form of Anthony. The name's great and continuing popularity is comparatively recent and originated from the cult of St Anthony of Padua (1195–1231), the Portuguese Franciscan. It was originally the Roman *nomen* Antonius, as in Cleopatra's friend Marcus Antonius. One famous holder of the name was the blind Mayo poet Antaine Ó Reachtabhra (1784–1835) who wrote among many other poems '*Mise Raifteirí an File*'.

AODH

[Also Áed] The word means 'fire' and is taken without warranty as the Irish version of the English name Hugh. In the form Áed, it was a very common name in early Ireland. A number of Irish saints were called by it and in the early seventeenth century it was the name given to the twin thorns in Elizabeth I's side: Aodh Ó Néill of Tír Eogháin and Aodh Ruadh Ó Dónaill of Tír Conaill.

ARDAL (ARDGHAL)

The name may mean 'great valour' or 'notable warrior' and is most commonly found in County Monaghan, where it was a popular forename with MacMahons and MacArdles. It is anglicised as Arnold.

ART

The word means 'bear' but it is also used figuratively in names as meaning 'warrior'. In Britain it is used as a diminutive of Arthur but there is no connection, that word coming from the Latin *Artorius* or *Artos* and referring to the mythic hero of Camelot. Art appears in semi-mythical form as the high king father of Cormac, the patron of the Fianna.

BARRY (BARRA)

A name in its own right but now most frequently used as a pet form of Finnbarr. At the time when biblical names were common it (like Bart) was a relief diminutive of Bartholomew.

BRENDAN (BREANDÁN)

[Also Brénainn] The name came from Wales when *breenhin* ('prince') was latinised into Brendanus and imported into Ireland at the time of the establishment of Irish monasticism. Of the many Irish saints who bore the name the most famous is the Tralee-born Brendan the Voyager (*c.* 486–578) who founded the monastery of Clonfert and whose name is associated with the tenth-century wonder tale *Brendan's Voyage*. The name enjoys a wide popularity but Kerry claims it; the county's diocesan college is Coláiste Bhréanainn.

BRIAN

Still one of the most common of Irish forenames and often taken, without linguistic authority, as an Irish form of Bernard and Barnaby. (Many Brians find themselves jocosely referred to as Barney.) The origin and meaning are obscure but it is Celtic and common in Britain with the spelling Bryan. In mythology Brian was the eldest of the three sons of Tureann, who were the Celtic equivalents of the Greek Argonauts. The first of the Irish worthies to hold the name was Brian Boru, who broke the power of the Scandinavians at Clontarf in 1014.

CAHAL (CATHAL)

The name means 'strong in battle' and was a popular name in the middle ages, held by kings of Munster and Connacht. It is taken without warranty as the Irish equivalent of Charles. Interestingly, though, the Young Pretender, Prince Charles Stuart, was known correctly as *Séarlas Óg*. Except in Ulster it is a monosyllable.

CAHIR (CATHAÍR)

[Also Cathaoir] The *cath* part of the name is the Irish word for 'battle' which suggests that the word means 'warrior'. The name continues to be popular in the northwest.

CANICE (CAINNEACH)

The name of the patron saint of places as far apart as Limavady and Kilkenny (which clearly bears his name). The word means 'pleasant, handsome', and since Canice was not only a Pict but travelled to Scotland with Colum Cille, the name is the source of the Scots name Kenneth.

CIAN

[Also Kean and Kian] The word in Irish can mean 'distance', 'time' and 'sorrow' but usually is taken as a name to signify 'ancient'. In mythology Cian was the son of Dian Cécht, the god of medicine, and seduced Ethlinn the daughter of Balor of Tory in spite of her imprisonment in a crystal tower on the island. Their son was the sun-god Lugh, father of Cúchulainn. The name was popular with the Monaghan clan MacMahon.

CIARAN

[Also Kieran and Kieron] The name means 'dark' or 'swarthy' and remains widely popular. The most famous St Ciaran (*c.* 516–*c.* 549) was the founder of the great monastic city of Clonmacnoise on the Shannon though he survived only for a short while afterwards. One of the earliest of the post-penal clerical seminaries was St Kieran's in Kilkenny.

CILLIAN

[Also Cillene and Killian] The name is clearly associated with the word *cill* ('church') and a suitable name for a saint. The best known is the seventh-century Cavan-born Kilian of Würzburg (in Bavaria) who was martyred with other Irish missionaries by Geilana, the wife of the convert Duke Gozbert.

COLE (COMGHALL)

[Also Cowal] The word means 'fellow-hostage' and was the name of the founder of the monastery of Bangor in County Down. Comgall (517–603) was a colleague of Colum Cille and the teacher of Columban and Gall who did so much to rekindle the faith in Europe in the sixth century.

COLIN (COILÍN)

The name may mean 'pup' and it is taken in Ireland as a diminutive of Colman. As such it is found mainly in the west and northwest. In Scotland it is widespread and it is popular too in England where it is regarded as a diminutive of Nicholas.

COLM

[Also Colum, Columb] The word is the equivalent of the Latin *columba* meaning 'dove', the Old Testament symbol of peace, and also associated with the Holy Spirit. The Tír Conaill saint (521–97) who founded many monasteries including Iona was called Colum Cille ('dove of the church'). This Scots connection resulted in the names Calum and Malcolm ('disciple of Colm').

COLMAN

A diminutive form of Colm and meaning 'pigeon'. It is the name of hundreds of Irish saints, most notably Colman of Lindisfarne. As the third abbot of Aidan's monastery at Lindisfarne, he refused to accept the rulings of the Synod of Whitby (664) which decreed that the Celtic church come into line with Rome. He stormed off with a group of Irish and English monks to set up a monastery in Connacht in a region thereafter known as *Muigheo na Sacsan* ('Mayo of the Saxons').

CONALL

[Also Connell] The word means 'strong as a wolf' and the name is one of the oldest in Ireland. Conall Cearnach was foster brother to Cúchulainn and in historical times Conall was one of the two sons of Niall of the Nine Hostages, the semi-mythological king who is said to have ruled AD 379–405 and who gave his name to Tír Conaill. One of several saints who bore the name was Conall of Iniskeel (an island off Portnoo in Donegal), now the patron saint of Glenties.

CONN

The word means 'sense' or 'reason' in Irish and the name therefore probably signifies 'wise head'. In mythology Conn was one of the children of Lir who were turned into swans by their wicked stepmother Aoife. In 'history' Conn of the Hundred Battles, who reigned AD 177–212, gave his name to Connacht.

CONOR (CONCHÚR)
[Also Conner and Connor] One of the oldest and currently among the most popular of Irish names. An early Conor, the mythological Conchobhar Mac Nessa was the founder of the Red Branch Knights, builder of Emain Macha and execrated betrothed of Deirdre. The name is associated, without warranty, with Cornelius, which appears in many other forms including Corny, Nelius, Neil and even Conn.

CORMAC
The word is taken to be a combination of *corb* ('defile') and *mac* ('son'). It was the name of the semi-historical Cormac Mac Art who is said to have ruled in the period AD 254–77. His name is linked to that of Fionn Mac Cumhail, who managed the Fianna as a kind of royal bodyguard.

DAHY (DÁITHÍ)

The word means 'the swift one' and the name is associated with Nathy (Náithí). One of that name, a nephew of Niall of the Nine Hostages, was a king of Connacht. In its Irish form it is confusingly taken as a translation of the Hebrew name David, which means 'beloved', though the correct version of that name is Dáibhéid which in turn is shortened to Dáibhí and pronounced like its English translation, Davy. This was the form used by the great seventeenth-century Irish poet Dáibhí Ó Bruadair.

DECLAN (DEAGLÁN)

The name, which is that of a pre-Patrician missionary to Ireland, has associations with 'light' or 'gleam'. The saint known as the 'Patrick of the Decies' is associated with Ardmore, County Waterford.

DERMOT (DIARMAID)

[Also Dermod, Diarmait, Diarmuid] The name has been taken to mean 'free of envy' but there is no general agreement. In Celtic mythology it was the name of the lover of Gráinne, Diarmuid Ó Duibhne ('Dermot of the Love Spot'). Their flight from Gráinne's husband Fionn Mac Cumhail forms the theme of the great mythic tale *Tóraigheacht Dhiarmada agus Ghráinne*. It was also the name of the king of Leinster, Dermot MacMurrough, who first brought the Normans to Ireland. A common diminutive is Derry.

DONAGH (DONNCHA)

[Also Donnchadh] A name of continuing popularity which means 'brown lord'. It is taken as the Irish equivalent of Denis or Dionysius, as usual in these cases without authority. It was the name of Brian Boru's eldest son and of several kings of Munster. It is also the source of the name Donat.

DONAL (DOMHNALL)

The name means 'world-almighty' and is often shortened to Donie. In mythology Domnhall was the Scot who taught Cúchulainn the finer arts of war. The name is still common in Scotland as Donald. Though it is taken universally as the Irish translation of the English Daniel, there is no connection. The name gave rise to the O'Donnell clan of Donegal and the MacDonnells of Antrim and Galloway.

DOUGLAS (DUBHGHLAS)

The word is made up of two colours, *dubh* (black) and *glas* (green). The name is Irish but it travelled to Scotland at a period when there was no linguistic difference between the countries and has remained a popular name. The Douglas clan supplied lieutenants to both Wallace (*c.* 1274–1305) and Robert Bruce (1274–1329) in their fights with the English. It was the name of the first president of Ireland, Douglas Hyde (1860–1949).

DUALTA (DUBHALTACH)

The word means 'dark-limbed' and is not common outside of Connacht and northwest Ulster. The most famous holder of the name was Dubaltach Mac Fir Bisigh (d. 1670), the seventeenth-century historian, known as the last of the Gaelic scholars.

EAMON(N) (ÉAMANN)

The Irish form of Edmund that came with the Anglo-Normans and means 'rich protection'. It was held by the ninth-century East Anglian king and martyr who gave his name to Bury St Edmunds. It is now taken as equivalent to Edward and is instantly recognised in Britain because of the television personality Eamonn Andrews (1922–87).

EGAN (AOGÁN)

[Also Aodhagán] The name is a pet form of Aidan and means 'little flame'. It was the name of the great Sliabh Luachra poet Aogán Ó Raithaille (1675–1729) and is also common in Ireland as a surname.

EMMET (EIMÉID)

There is no true Gaelic equivalent for this name since its use as a forename is entirely as a tribute to Robert Emmet (1778–1803), the patriot whose romantic love for Sarah Curran led to his capture after his abortive Dublin rising in the year of his death.

ENDA (ÉANNA)

The first syllable *éan* is the Irish word for 'bird' so the name could mean 'birdlike'. It is found in Enna Airgthetch, a legendary king of Munster, who distributed silver shields to his warriors. Historically Enda is one of the great names of early Irish monasticism. He was trained at the famous 'white house' of Ninian on the Solway Firth and is believed to have established the first Irish monastery, on Inis Mór in the Aran Islands. He died there *c.* 530.

EOGHAN

The word means 'born of the yew' and the name occurs often in mythology, most dramatically in the case of Eoghan, son of Durthacht, who killed the sons of Usna and who was driving the chariot out of which Deirdre killed herself. Eoghan of Ardstraw, County Tyrone, was an early monastic founder and is patron of the diocese of Derry. The name has been done into English as Eugene ('well-born'). Other forms are Owen and Owain (the Welsh form of Eugene).

EOIN

The older Irish equivalent of John and the name used for the evangelist. It derives directly from the Latin *Johannes*. The more common modern name Seán came from French with the Anglo-Normans. Like all its European equivalents it remains a very popular name.

ERNAN (EARNÁN)

The word has connections with *iarann* ('iron') and may be cognate with Erannán, the Milesian who fell to his death from the mast of his father's ship at his first sight of Ireland. St Earnán is the patron saint of Tory Island off the Donegal coast. The name is taken as the Irish form of Ernest.

EUNAN (ÁDHAMHNÁN)

[Also Adomnán] The name of the biographer of Colum Cille and his successor as abbot of Iona. The word means 'fretful one' and as such is inappropriate to its bearer. He was born in Raphoe in 624 and is the patron saint of that diocese. He succeeded in establishing an early 'Geneva Convention' for the treatment of women, children and clerics in time of war and was foremost in persuading the Irish to accept the decrees of the Synod of Whitby (664) which brought the Celtic church into alignment with Rome. The name is now current mainly in the north of Ireland.

FERGAL (FEARGHAL)

The word means 'man of strength' and has been a popular name in Ireland since earliest times. St Fergal of Aghaboe (aka Virgil) was famous as a 'geometer' and was the unordained bishop of eighth-century Salzburg for forty-four years until his death in 784. The name is the source of the surname Farrell.

FERGUS (FEARGHUS)

The word has connotations of strength and masculinity, and it is a very ancient Irish name. It is held by many Irish heroes, notably Fergus Mac Roth who is an important figure in the *Táin Bó Cuailgne* the great Ulster saga. In the sixth century Fergus Mac Erc led an army of Irish, then known as Scoti, to colonise Argyll and thus gave the title to modern Scotland. The name is still very popular there and in northern England.

FIACRE (FIACHRA)

The word is connected with *fiach* ('raven'). Fiachra was one of the children of Lir, a brother of Conn and Fionnuala. The name is shared with the French four-wheeled cabs that made their appearance in Paris in 1620 and had their stand opposite the Hôtel Saint-Fiacre. Saint Fiachra was from Bangor and became one of the premier saints of France and patron of gardeners because of the excellence of the vegetables which grew round his hermitage at Meaux. He died there in 670.

FINAN (FÍONÁN)

The word has connections with the Irish *fíon* ('wine') and was the name of a decade of Irish saints, most notably Finan of Lindisfarne who succeeded Aidan and was a strong supporter of Celtic church practices against those of Rome. He died in 661, three years before these matters were settled at the Synod of Whitby.

Finn (Fionn)

The word means 'fair' and is of course the name of the great Irish mythological hero Fionn Mac Cumhail, the founder and leader of the Fianna. The volcanic cooling which resulted in the natural wonders of the Giant's Causeway in County Antrim and in the Hebridean Isle of Staffa are credited to the Irish Finn and his Scots rival Fingal ('fair stranger') when as giants they each agreed to build a causeway to facilitate a challenge.

Fin(n)barr (Fionnbharr)

The word means 'fair-haired' and it was the name of one of the Tuatha Dé Danann, the divine race who inhabited Ireland before the coming of the Milesians. There were several Irish saints called Fionnbhar, the most influential being the patron saint of Cork. He established a hermitage at Gougane Barra (*Gúgán Barra* – 'Barra's Creek') near the source of the Lee, but on angelic instruction followed the river to the present position of the city and established a monastery there. He died *c.* 633.

FINTAN (FIONNTÁN)

The name means 'white ancient' and is that of the famous Salmon of Knowledge which gave Fionn Mac Cumhail's thumb such power. It was also the name of one of the sons of Niall of the Nine Hostages and of a number of saints, notably Fintan of Cloneenagh, County Laois, who, in spite of the extreme austerity of his rule and a diet of stale barley bread and muddy water, was known for his handsome, healthy appearance. Another Fintan (aka Findan) was captured by Vikings and taken off to their Orkney stronghold. He escaped and went on a thanksgiving pilgrimage to Rome. On his road home he stopped at Rheinau in Switzerland and lived there as a recluse for the remainder of his life. He died in 878.

FLANN

The word means 'blood red' and may be used as a girl's name. Flann Mac Dima, a semi-mythological character, had an affair with the wife of a high king Diarmuid who reigned 545–68. He drowned in a water tank trying to escape from the burning house that Diarmuid had set on fire. Flann Sinna, who reigned as high king for thirty-six years, died in 916 and is commemorated on King Flann's high cross at Clonmacnoise.

FLANNAN (FLANNÁN)

A pet form of Flann. It is the name of the saint who christened the Flannan Isles in the Outer Hebrides and is the patron saint of the diocese of Killaloe and of the diocesan seminary in Ennis.

GARRET (GEARÓID)
[Also Gearalt] The name is essentially Anglo-Norman, coming in with Strongbow and settling happily. It is anglicised as Gerard and as Gerald, a form not so common in Ireland but the usual one in Britain. The original word was Germanic and meant 'hard as a spear', and with the prefix 'Fitz' (the Norman word to correspond with the Irish 'Mac', though usually indicating illegitimacy) it became the surname of the greatest Norman-Irish family.

GARVIN (GARBHÁN)
The word means 'rough' (from the Irish *garbh*) and the name was that of several saints. It is more common as a surname.

JARLATH (IARLAITH)

The name of the patron saint of the archdiocese of Tuam, who was chosen as Patrick's successor in Armagh. According to tradition, in old age he was taken by his pupil Brendan of Clonfert in a chariot to find an appropriate place to spend his few remaining years. A wheel broke at Tuam and there the old man died *c.* 550.

KEVIN (CAOIMHÍN)

The word means 'handsome child' and was the name of the great founder (d. 618) of the monastery at Glendalough, County Wicklow. The wonder tales associated with the saint emphasise the love of wild nature that was characteristic of the early monks.

Labhrás

The word is Irish for laurel, which makes it an appropriate Irish form of Laurence (*Laurentius*) which means 'one from Laurentum' (a lost Roman town). It was one of the forms given by the Irish chroniclers to the Leinster saint usually called Laurence O'Toole (*c.* 1130–80).

Liam

The name was originally *Uilliam*, the Irish form of William, which came with the Anglo-Normans and became popular throughout Ireland when the invaders became 'more Irish than the Irish themselves'. William is Teutonic in origin and combines the elements 'will' and 'helmet'. The form Liam has completely superseded William and is a very popular name for Irish boys. It has also recently become current in Britain.

LOCHLANN

The word means 'Scandinavian' and was applied to the invaders during the period (ninth and tenth centuries) of the Viking raids and mercantile colonisation. In time it became a common surname in the northwest. The form Lachlan (shortened to Lachie) is common in Scotland, while the English version Laughlin has Lockie as its diminutive.

LORCÁN

The word means 'fierce' but it was the name of Ireland's first canonised (1226) saint, Lorcán Ó Tuathail, anglicised as Laurence O'Toole, who acted as a go-between for the Irish and Strongbow's Anglo-Norman adventurers.

MALACHY (MAOILSEACHLAINN)

The English form of the name comes from the Old Testament Malachi, one of the prophets, and means 'my messenger'. It became popular in Ireland because of two saints, Maolmaodhog (1094–1148), the reforming archbishop of Armagh, and Sechnall, one of St Patrick's first converts. A disciple of the latter was known as Máel Sechnaill and it became a popular name in Leinster. The Malachy who 'wore the collar of gold/That he won from the proud invader' in Thomas Moore's song 'Let Erin Remember' was Máel Sechnaill Mór Mac Domhnaill.

MANUS (MÁNUS)

[Also Maghnus] The name, from the Latin *magnus* ('great'), came to Ireland in tribute to Carolus Magnus (742–814), the first Holy Roman Emperor, better known as Charlemagne. His court at Aachen was the centre of an early renaissance of learning and art, his teachers coming mainly from Ireland. The name became largely confined to the northwest, where it is still to be found.

MICHEÁL

From Michael ('who is like the Lord?'), the name of the premier archangel and one of the biblical borrowings like John and Mary that inevitably found Gaelic equivalents among a Christian people. It became as prevalent as Patrick in the last two centuries and its diminutive Mick, like Paddy, became a generic name for Irish immigrants in Britain, America and Australia. In the British Army the Irish Guards are known as the 'Micks'.

MUIRIS

The Irish form of Maurice from the Latin *Mauricius* which means 'dark-skinned' i.e. Moorish. It has also assimilated the native Irish name Muirgheas which means 'sea-strength'. The original Maurice, a Christian officer, was martyred with all his men in Switzerland in the fifth century for refusing to take part in heathen sacrifice.

NAOISE
The eldest of the three sons of Usna and lover of Deirdre, the betrothed of Conchobhar Mac Nessa. It was not much used as a name historically but has become popular with the revival of interest in Celtic mythology. It is taken as the Gaelic form of Noah.

NEIL (NIALL)
The word may mean 'cloud' or 'champion' and became a name popular with kings and clan chieftains largely because of the fame of the semi-mythological Niall of the Nine Hostages. It gave rise to the surnames MacNeill and O'Neill. It is if anything more popular in Scotland. It was latinised as Nigellus which in turn produced the popular English name Nigel.

NOLLAIG
The Irish form of Noel from the Latin *natalis* ([Christ's] 'birthday'). It has had some popularity in recent years and is used also as a girl's name, translating Noëlle.

OISÍN

The word means 'little deer' and refers to the story that Oisín, the son of Sadhbh by Fionn Mac Cumhail, was reared in the forest by his mother, who had been turned into a doe. Fionn found him and, hearing his story, claimed him as his son and made him an important member of the Fianna, who excelled both as warrior and poet. The English form is Ossian.

OLIVER (OILIBHÉAR)

The name is not Irish but cognate with the Teutonic Olaf. Its popularity in Ireland is entirely ascribable to Archbishop Oliver Plunkett (1625–81) who was executed at Tyburn for treason and canonised in 1975. Since it was the forename of Cromwell, Ireland's greatest Satan, it ceased to be popular until 1920, when Plunkett was beatified.

ORAN (ODHRÁN)

The word means 'sallow' and of many saints who bore the name the most significant was Patrick's charioteer. There is on Iona a St Oran's well and it is believed than a saint of that name may have been there before Colum Cille.

OSCAR (OSGAR)

The word means 'deer lover' and in spite of its Scandinavian appearance the name is authentically Irish – as was its most famous holder Oscar Wilde (1854–1900). It was exported to the land of the Norsemen and has remained very popular, especially in Sweden, where it is spelt Oskar. Oscar was the son of Oisín and, though initially noted for his clumsiness, became the mightiest warrior of all the Fianna.

PATRICK (PÁDRAIG)

This quintessential Irish name is of course Latin, *Patricius* meaning 'noble', and is not confined to Ireland. It is to be found widely in Britain and in France. Since the British saint who established Christianity as the national religion was held in deep reverence the name was not given to children for hundreds of years after his death, except in such forms as *Giolla Pátraic*, 'servant of Patrick'. Its widespread popularity is less than three hundred years old. It has many forms both in English and Irish, though the most common diminutive, Paddy, like Mick, may now in certain contexts smack of racism.

PEADAR

The Irish form of the biblical Peter which was the Greek translation of the Aramaic *Cephas* meaning 'rock'. It was as popular in Ireland as elsewhere in Europe since its source was so important a saint of the church.

PEARSE (PIARAS)
[Also Piers, Pierce] The name is a form of Peter but its popularity in Ireland is almost entirely due to Patrick H. Pearse (1879–1916) the leader of the Easter Rising.

PHELIM (FEIDHLIM)
[Also Felim] The word may mean 'always good' and the name itself is very ancient. Felim (aka Fedilmid) was the father of Deirdre, the tragic lover of Naoise and betrothed of Conchobhar Mac Nessa. It was also the name of Colum Cille's father and as such is most commonly found in Donegal.

PILIB
The Irish form of Philip, which comes from the Greek and means lover of horses. It arrived in Ireland with the Anglo-Normans and in time produced the common Scots surname MacKillop.

PÓL

The Irish version of Paul from the Latin *paulus* meaning 'small'. It was the name taken by Saul of Tarsus after Damascus. As with Peter the name is of recent popularity, having received a boost with the elevation of Paul VI (1897–1978) to the papacy in 1963.

PROINSIAS

[Also Proinnsias] The Irish form of Francis which is from the medieval Latin *Franciscus* meaning 'French'. As with many other saints' names the source of its popularity was essentially devotional, in this case to St Francis of Assisi (1181–1226).

RANDAL (RAGHNAL)
A borrowing from the Norse name Ragnvald which means 'ruler's decision'. It is used also as a form of the English Randolph which means 'wolf shield'. It remains a popular name in County Antrim.

REDMOND (RÉAMANN)
The Irish form of Raymond which means 'protector', and which was a common Norman name, coming to Ireland with Strongbow's adventurers. The last Catholic bishop of Derry until after the relaxation of the Penal Laws was Redmond O'Gallagher (murdered 1601).

RISTEÁRD
The Irish form of Richard which came with the Normans and became popular. It means 'strong ruler' a description that was not exactly appropriate for the three English kings who bore the name.

RONAN (RÓNÁN)

From the Gaelic word *rón* meaning 'seal', it was the name of the Irish equivalent of Theseus in the myth of Phaedra. Ronan's second wife fell guiltily in love with her stepson Mael Fhothartaigh. Rebuffed, she lied to her husband about him and the son was killed on the orders of his father, who afterwards died of grief when he found out the truth. It was also the name of the saint who cursed Suibhne Geilt in the poem *Buile Suibne*.

RORY (RUAIRÍ)

[Also Ruaidhrí] The word means 'red king' and is sometimes taken as equivalent to Roderick. It was the name of the last high king of Ireland, Rory O'Connor, who made peace with Henry II, and of a noted opponent of the English, Rory Oge O'More (d. 1578).

RYAN (RÍAN)

Though used mainly now as a surname, Rían meaning 'little king' was the name of several saints and warriors. Its use as a forename is more common outside Ireland.

SEAMUS (SÉAMAS)

[Also (older) Seumas] The Irish translation of James, an historical necessity thanks to Ireland's fateful involvement with the unreliable Stuarts. Since it is a biblical name and existed in most European countries it was inevitable that Ireland should devise its own form. It was common among the Anglo-Norman settlers for the same reasons. It appears in Scotland as Hamish (like most anglicised Scottish names a vocative) and is still a widely popular name in both countries. It is often reduced to Shay.

SEAN (SEÁN)

[Also (older) Seaghan] As with Seamus, Ireland needed its own equivalent of the universal John, though Eoin, the early biblical version, would have served. The agreed form of the Irish spelling is comparatively recent but the name's association with the French Jean which was brought by the Anglo-Normans meant that the name prospered with a parallel career to Eoin.

Seathrún

The Irish version of Geoffrey (Old High German meaning 'district peace') and relatively uncommon on that account. One worthy holder of the name was the poet and historian Seathrún Céitinn (*c.* 1580–*c.* 1644) who wrote *Foras Feasa ar Éirinn* (1629–34), the history of a Gaelic Ireland that was suffering apocalyptic change.

Senan (Seanán)

The word has its root in an Old Irish word meaning 'wise'. The name is usually associated with County Clare largely because the most famous holder of the name, the sixth-century Senan of Kilrush, ruled an important monastery at Scattery Island (Inis Cathaigh) on the Shannon estuary.

Seosamh

The more usual Irish version of the biblical Joseph ('God increases') though the husband of the Blessed Virgin would be referred to by an older form, Iosep, widely in use in pre-Norman times.

SHANE
An anglicised (and usually northern) form of
Sean.

SORLEY (SOMHAIRLE)
An Ulster name that comes from the Old Norse
and means 'summer wanderer'. The name was
popular with the MacDonnells of Dalraida, the
Scots-Irish kingdom which regarded the North
Channel as central to its territory. In the sixteenth
century Somhairle Buí Mac Domhnaill (1505–90)
was a recurrent thorn in the side of Elizabeth I.

TADHG

The word means 'poet' and is also used to translate 'the man in the street': *Tadhg an mhargaidh* (lit. 'Tadgh of the market'). It was, however, the name of several ancient kings of Ireland. It is used as the Irish equivalent of the English Timothy (from the Greek 'God-honoured'). The form Taig is used as an anti-Catholic form of abuse by Loyalists in the North, while an older form Teague was the standard stage name for an Irishman.

TIERNAN (TIARNÁN)

A word meaning 'lord'. The name, although usually associated with the surname O'Rourke, is steadily gaining a wider popularity.

TOMÁS

The Irish version of Thomas, the biblical name meaning 'twin', and required for ecclesiastical purposes like Peter, John and the rest. This form is as popular in Ireland as its equivalents throughout Europe.

TURLOUGH (TRAOLACH)

[Also Tarlach] The name, which in its older Irish form Toirdhealbhach means 'aider' or 'abettor', was borne by a number of kings. It was also the name of the blind harper and composer Turlough O'Carolan (1670–1732). The Irish form of the name is taken as a translation of Terence.

UINSEANN

The Irish form of Vincent, which is from the Latin and means 'conquering'. Its awkward look and difficult pronunciation have not helped its popularity. It is usually to be found where the Irish form of a family name has been preferred.

ULTAN (ULTÁN)

The name means 'Ulsterman' and was the name of several saints, most notably the *peregrinus* brother of Fursa and Foillán who died as abbot of Peronne on the Somme in 686.

NAMES FOR GIRLS

AILBHE (AILBE)

The word may mean 'white' or 'fair'. Ailbe Gruadbrec ('freckled cheeks') was a daughter of Cormac Mac Airt and the much appreciated mistress of Fionn Mac Cumhail, whose lover she became after correctly answering a set of riddles (an early example of marrying the boss's daughter). The name is also that of several male saints, most notably Ailbe of Emly.

AILIS (AILÍS)

The Irish equivalent of Alice which came with the Anglo-Normans and meant 'noble'. It is also used as an alternative spelling for Eilís which is more correctly the Irish version of Elizabeth. The fourteenth-century witch of Kilkenny, Dame Kyteler, was one notorious bearer of the name.

ÁINE

The word means 'brightness' and was once also a male name. In mythology Áine was the goddess of love and fertility, the daughter of the foster son of the sea-god Manannán Mac Lir (another resemblance to Aphrodite). The name's formal similarity to the Hebrew Anna ('God has favoured me') has led to its being taken as a translation but there is no linguistic connection. Enya, the name of the popular singer and composer, is a phonetic approximation to the Donegal pronunciation of Áine.

AINGEAL

The Irish form of the English Angela, from the Greek and meaning 'messenger' – which was what an angel was.

AISLING

The word means 'vision' and is applied to the seventeenth and eighteenth-century verse of such poets as Aogán Ó Raithaille in which a sorrowful Ireland appears as a beautiful woman. The name is comparatively recent but phonically and otherwise entirely appropriate as a girl's name.

ALANNAH

The word is a nineteenth-century transliteration of the vocative, '*A leanbh*'('Child!'). Its pleasant sound is its main recommendation as a name. It is not a feminine form of Alan, though sometimes treated as such.

AOIBHEANN

[Also Aoibhinn] The word means 'blissful' and only recently regained an early popularity. It is anglicised as Eavan.

AOIFE

The word means 'beautiful' and the name occurs in several places in Irish mythology. One notorious Aoife was Lir's second wife, who was so cruel to Fionnuala and her cygnet brothers. Another in historical times was the wife of Strongbow. Because of the similarity of sound it was taken as a translation of Eva and (Mother) Eve, the usual Irish version of which is Éabha.

ATTRACTA (ATHRACHT)

A name less popular now than at the turn of the century. Little is known of St Attracta except that she gave her name to Killaraght in County Mayo. There is a legend that she ran away from home to become a nun and was given the veil by Patrick himself, but this story shows little acquaintance with the true nature of Irish monasticism.

BÁIRBRE

The Irish form of Barbara which is Greek and means 'foreigner'. St Barbara is one of the saints of the early church who, like Philomena and Christopher, have been derogated, not to say abolished, by Vatican II. In the story her father, attempting to put her to death because she refused to renounce Christianity, was reduced to ashes by a lightning bolt. She became the patron of artillerymen, among other flashy types.

BERNADETTE (BEARNAIRDÍN)

The name became extremely popular in Ireland because of the 1858 appearances of the Virgin Mary at Lourdes to Marie Bernarde Soubirous (1844–79), especially after her canonisation in 1933. The Irish name is a diminutive of the Irish form of Bernard, as indeed was Bernadette of the French. The English name is shortened in Ireland to Berna and Detta.

BLANAID (BLÁTHNÁIT)

The word means 'little flower' and one bearer of the name was wife of the Munster king Cú Roí and lover of Cúchulainn. The form Bláithín is used to translate the pet name of St Thérèse of Lisieux.

BRIGID (BRÍD)

[Also Bridget, Brigit, Bride, Bridín *et al*] The word means 'high-goddess' and in mythology she had a triune nature as goddess of healing, fertility and smiths. Her festival Imbolc (held on 1 February) marked the beginning of the Celtic spring. Brigid is also the name of the greatest of Irish woman saints and the cults of the goddess and the saint have often become confused. The historical Brigid (who may have been a priestess of the goddess) was born in Faughart, County Louth, *c.* 450 and died in her great foundation in Kildare *c.* 523. The custom of plaiting crosses for her feast (also 1 February) is probably a carry-over from the cult of the goddess.

BRONAGH (BRÓNACH)

The words means 'sorrowful' and so serves as an Irish version of Dolores. Brónach was a saint, a patron of seafarers who is celebrated in Kilbroney near Rostrevor (County Down), where there is a St Brónach's Well.

CAOILFHIONN
[Also Caoilinn] The word is formed of a combination of two Irish words meaning 'slender' and 'fair' and the name deserves its place on grounds of euphony alone. It was the name of several Irish saints.

CAOIMHE
The word means 'beauty' or 'grace' and it was the name of a saint who may have given her name to Killeavy in south Armagh.

CARMEL (CAIRMEÁL)
The name comes from Our Lady of Mount Carmel (the hill in Syria associated with the prophet Elijah) and the inspiration for the order of twelfth-century mendicants known also as Whitefriars. The name is rarely found outside Ireland and it was popular especially where there was a Carmelite foundation.

CATRIONA (CAITRÍONA)

The Irish form of Catherine, meaning 'pure', became popular after the Crusades when colourful stories of Catherine of Alexandria, the fourth-century virgin-martyr, were brought home, although she who gave her name to the firework probably never existed. The shortened forms, Cáit, Triona and Riona became very popular, the latter two more common in Scotland.

CIANA

Female form of the boy's name Cian. In mythology her name is associated with storms at sea.

CIARA

Associated with Ciar, a feminine version of Ciaran, the word means 'dark' or 'black'. To add to the confusion Ciara is also the Italian for Clare, which means 'bright' or 'clear'. The name is growing steadily in popularity, as much for reasons of euphony as significance.

CLIONA (CLÍODHNA)
The name of a goddess of beauty who lived in
the Land of Promise, where Oisín and Niamh
spent three hundred years in dalliance. She fell
in love with a mortal, Ciabhán of the Curling
Locks, and escaped with him to Glandore in
County Cork. Clíodhna's father then persuaded
Manannán Mac Lir to waft her back home on
a huge wave. In later stories she is a kind of
resident house fairy to the MacCarthys.

CLODAGH
The name of a tributary of the River Suir, one
of several of that name in the southeast. A
Marquis of Waterford chose it as a name for one
of his daughters and its popularity dates from
then.

COLLEEN
The international version of the Irish word
cailín which means 'girl', 'unmarried woman'.
The name is rather more popular in the US and
Australia than at home.

IRISH NAMES FOR CHILDREN

DAMHNAIT

The word means 'fawn' and is taken, without much authority, as the Irish version of Dympna. St Dympna, who is venerated in Gheel, near Antwerp, was supposed to be the daughter of a pagan Irish prince who when his wife died conceived an incestuous passion for her. She fled to Gheel but was followed by her father who killed her. She has since become the patron of the insane. Tydavnet (Damhnait's House) in County Monaghan is the site of a convent founded by a sixth-century Damhnait.

DANA

The less-used name of the goddess Danu, the presiding deity of the Tuatha Dé Danann, the supernatural race who lived in Ireland before the coming of the Milesians. The word means 'abundance' but it is confused with *dána* (meaning 'audacious').

DARINA (DÁIRÍNE)

The word means 'fruitful' and it was the name of the younger daughter of the High King Tuathal Teachthmair, who married Eochaidh, king of Leinster, on the death of his first wife, her sister Fithir. When she arrived at her husband's castle she discovered Fithir was still alive. Both women died of shame.

DEIRDRE

The name of the most famous woman in Irish mythology, the betrothed of Conchobhar Mac Nessa, who loved Naoise, the eldest of the three sons of Usna, and on his treacherous death dashed her head against a rock rather than live with Conchobhar. She has fascinated many poets and writers since the anonymous chroniclers of *Longes mac nUislenn* ('Exile of the Sons of Uisliu') in the Ulster cycle first recorded her story, most notably in the unfinished *Deirdre of the Sorrows* (1910) by J. M. Synge.

DERVLA (DEARBHÁIL)

The word may mean 'daughter of Fál' (a legendary name for Ireland) or 'true desire'. In modern times it has been associated with Deirbhile ('poet's daughter') and the English form has been re-spelt as Dearbhla. Deirbhile was a sixth-century Mayo saint.

DOIREANN

The word may mean 'daughter of Fionn' but in mythology Doirend was the daughter of Bodb Dearg, the son of the Dagda. It is used as a translation of Doreen but there is no basis except usage for regarding it as an equivalent of the English Dorothy.

EILÍS
The best equivalent for Elizabeth ('God is satisfied'), a name with more diminutives than any other. The name, like so many others, came into Ireland with the Anglo-Normans, sometimes in its Spanish form, Isobel. It remains, of course, very popular.

EITHNE
[Also Ethna] The word may mean 'whin' and of many who bore the name in Irish mythology the best known is the Ethniu who was imprisoned in a crystal tower in Tory Island and bore a child to Cian, Lugh, who became god of the sun and of arts and crafts. It was also the name of Colum Cille's mother.

EILEEN (EIBHLÍN)
[Also Aileen, Aibhlín] The name came with the Anglo-Normans as Evelyn, Evalina and Emmeline but soon acquired an Irish form. The original was a diminutive of Eve ('life').

EMER (EIMHEAR)

The daughter of Forgall Manach of Leinster and wife of Cúchulainn. Though many other women played a part in his life, notably Fand, the wife of Manannán Mac Lir, the sea-god, it was always to Emer and Dún Dealgan that Cúchulainn returned.

ÉTÁIN

Of several Étáins in Celtic mythology the most fascinating is the one called 'the most beautiful woman in all Ireland'. The god Midir fell in love with her and won her with the help of Aengus, the love god. Midir took her to his home where, not unnaturally, she fell foul of Midir's wife, Fuamnach, who changed her in turn into a pool of water, a worm and a fly to confuse Midir in his search for her. There was a happy ending but not until after much travail. The word has associations with jealousy and is anglicised as Aidin, sometimes appearing as Aideen.

FANCHEA (FAINCHE)

[Also Fuinche] The name of many Irish saints, most notably Fanchea of Rossory on the Erne, near Enniskillen. She was a sister of the great father of Irish monasticism, Enda of Aran, and his main influence towards the religious life. The word means 'crow' and may have connections with the Morrigan, the Celtic goddess of war.

FIDELMA (FEIDHELM)

The name of several figures in Irish mythology, including a famous amazon warrior, Fidelma Noícrothach ('the nine-times beautiful'), the daughter of Conchobhar Mac Nessa and a woman of the Sí who fell in love with Cúchulainn. It was also the name of a number of saints.

FÍONA

The word comes from the Latin *vinea* ('vine') and has strictly speaking no connection with the Scots name Fiona which takes the stress on the second vowel. That name was invented by James Macpherson (1736–96) as a feminine form of Fionn in his 'translation' of the Fianna stories which he set solely in Scotland.

FIONNUALA

The word means 'fair-shouldered' and the Gaelic spelling is now more common than the still very popular (anglicised) Finola. In Irish legend Fionnuala was the daughter of Lir, the sea-god, turned with her brothers into a swan and condemned to nine hundred years of watery life by Aoife, her stepmother. The name is often shortened to Nuala and Nola and Sir Walter Scott has a form Fenella. In County Derry Finvola is popular.

GERALDINE (GEARÓIDÍN)

A generic name in romantic histories for the Earls of Kildare and applied by Henry Howard, Earl of Surrey (1517–47) to the daughter of the ninth earl: 'the fair Geraldine'. It was bound to become popular on grounds of euphony alone and in time an Irish form was devised.

GILEESA (GIOLLA ÍOSA)

The name, in theory applicable to both genders, means 'servant of Christ'. Because of its feminine ending it is now rarely given to boys. It is an example of the reverential ban on naming babies directly for Christ (also applied until modern times to Mary and Patrick) which seems to affect most European countries except Spain.

GRANIA (GRÁINNE)

The word could mean 'inspirer of terror' though *gráinne* in modern Irish means 'grain'. The combination suggests 'one who must be obeyed', a goddess of plenty. She was the 'fatal Cleopatra' for whom Diarmuid of the Love Spot thought the world well lost. The name is taken as a translation of Grace, which coming from the Latin *gratia* means what it says.

ITA (ÍDE)

The word means 'hunger' and may refer to the spiritual longing expressed by St Ita (died *c.* 570) for Christ. She founded an important convent in County Limerick, where traditionally one of her pupils was St Brendan, and left her name in Killeedy. According to legend she suckled the infant Jesus.

JOYCE (SEOIGHE)

Originally from the Breton 'lord' it comes from the Anglo-Norman surname, which was that of one of the Galway 'tribes'. Joy, ostensibly a diminutive, is probably a different, Quaker name.

KATHLEEN (CAITLÍN)

The name came from France as Cateline, after the probably fictitious Catherine of Alexandria, and was introduced by the Anglo-Normans. The Irish form is truer to the original but Kathleen, Kate and Kathy were and are still very popular. In the earliest version of Yeats's play that may have 'sent out certain men the English shot' the title was *Kathleen Ni Houlihan*. The Irish form is often shortened to Cáit.

KERRY

A tribute to euphony and Ireland's most colourful county, the name is steadily growing in popularity not only with natives of the 'kingdom' but wherever its reputation is known. If an Irish form is required the name of the county, Ciarraí, will serve.

LAOISE

[Also Laoiseach] The word probably means 'radiant girl' and, though there is no connection, often translates Louise, from Louis ('warrior') and Lucy, Lucia (both from the Latin *lux* meaning 'light').

LÁRA

The Irish version of Laura, which is Latin for 'laurel'. The diminutive Loretta is occasionally found in Ireland because of its similarity in sound to Loreto, the reputed house of Joseph and Mary in Nazareth which was miraculously translated to Italy in the thirteenth century and gave its name to an order of teaching nuns.

LASSARINA (LASAIRFHÍONA)

The word means 'flame of the wine', a romantic concept which endeared the name to the O'Connor family, where it was regularly given to daughters. Fíona may be a shortened form.

LÍADAN

The word means 'grey lady' and the original Líadan was an Irish Heloise who fell in love with Cuirithir, a poet like herself. Spurning him on a whim, she became a nun while he, heartbroken, became a monk. They both bitterly regretted their haste. Cuirithir was exiled and Líadan died after much sorrow on the stone he used as a prie-dieu. A poetic lament, as spoken by her, is extant in a ninth-century manuscript.

MAEVE (MEADHBH)

'She who intoxicates' was a goddess who in another incarnation became queen of Connacht, having taken Ailill the king as her fourth husband. She figures in the great epic of the *Táin Bó Cuailgne* ('The Cattle Raid of Cuailgne') which ended with the death of Cúchulainn. She makes an appearance as Mab, the fairy queen who figures so much in Mercutio's speech in Shakespeare's *Romeo and Juliet*.

MÁIRE

Out of reverence the name of the Blessed Virgin, like that of Patrick, was not given to children in early Ireland. As in all other countries in Europe, however, it became the most popular of all women's names. The form Muire is retained as the Virgin's name. The simple English Mary is now less common than it used to be but pet forms such as Maura and Maureen (Máirín) abound. The word comes from the Hebrew Miriam and may mean 'bitter'.

MAIRÉAD (MÁIRGHRÉAD)

The Irish form of Margaret, used at first in tribute to the saint who was the wife of St Malcolm, son of the murdered Duncan in Shakespeare's *Macbeth*. Its diminutives Peg and Peggy are written in Irish as Peig and Peigí. The word is Greek and means 'pearl'.

MAJELLA

The Italian surname of St Gerard, the Redemptorist lay-brother (1726–55), patron saint of mothers in childbirth. His canonisation in 1904 greatly increased the popularity of Gerard as a name for boys while the surname sounded right for girls.

MOLLY (MALLAIDH)

A pet name for Mary which became so identified as an Irish name that an Irish form was found for it. The name has figured in Ireland in song and story for the last three centuries, from Ms Malone with her barrow to Mrs Bloom with her fantasies with lots of Irish Molly-os thrown in for good measure.

MONA (MUADHNAIT)

The word means 'noble' and is guaranteed Irish. (The famous Leonardo da Vinci painting *La Gioconda* of 1504 is of a woman called correctly Monna Lisa.) St Muadhnait (of Drumcliffe) was a sister of the great saint Molaise who founded the monastery of Devenish. Mona is sometimes used as a diminutive of Monica.

MÓR

Meaning both 'tall' and 'great' in the figurative sense, the name was popular as a reverential substitute for the name of the Virgin. In Scotland it became Morag, a recognised diminutive and still a very popular name there. Móirín, the Irish diminutive, sounds so much like Máirín that they became confused.

MUIREANN

The word means 'sea-white' and figures in mythology as the name of the wife of Oisín. It was also that of the nurse of Cael, a warrior of the Fianna, who composed a wooing-poem so effective that it won for him Credhe, the daughter of the king of Kerry.

NÁBLA

[Also Nápla] The Irish version of Annabel which in turn probably came from Amabel from the Latin *amabilis* meaning 'lovable'. Like many names with a Latin origin it came into Ireland with the Anglo-Normans.

NESSA (NEASA)

The mother of Conchobhar who was mainly instrumental in making her son king of Ulster, thus increasing her own power. Another Nessa was the sister of St Ita. It is used as a pet name for Agnes and Vanessa.

NIAMH

The word means 'radiance' and the name appears as that of a Celtic goddess. Niamh Chinn Óir ('Niamh of the Golden Hair') was one of the daughters of the sea-god Manannán Mac Lir. She seduced Oisín into travelling with her to the Land of Promise and their three-week stay proved to have lasted three hundred earth-years. When Oisín returned and his foot touched the land of Ireland the full weight of his years came upon him.

NOËLLE (NOLLAIG)

The feminine form of Noel, the Christmas name, and having the same Irish spelling. The diminutive, Noeleen (also a diminutive of Nola), is rendered in Irish as Nollaigín.

NORA (NÓRA)

The name comes from Onóra, the Irish form of Honora which like Honor is Latin and speaks for itself. Long popular in Ireland and an identifiable Irish name, elsewhere its euphony caused an English version Norah to be devised. It is also taken as a sort form of Leonora and Eleanor. The popular diminutive Noreen has an Irish form Nóirín.

ÓRLA

[Also Órlaith, Orfhlaith] The word means 'golden princess' and was very common in pre-Norman Ireland. After a long period in eclipse it is now extremely popular again.

PATRICIA (PÁDRAIGÍN)

The old-fashioned patriot needed a female equivalent for Ireland's national apostle and so an early Latin name, the feminine form of Patricius, meaning 'noble', was devised. The Irish form is equally contrived.

PHILOMENA

The word is not so much a name as a quality, from the Greek and meaning 'loved one'. The cult of the saint did not begin until 1802 and the name became very popular throughout the church and *a fortiori* Ireland. The saint was one of the first to be derogated by Vatican II and the name has become less popular since.

REALTÁN (REAILTÍN)

The Irish version of Stella from the Latin meaning 'star'.

RÓISÍN

The diminutive of the Irish Róis from the English Rose which comes either from *hros* (Old German meaning 'horse') or *rosa* (Latin meaning 'rose'); it depends upon your romance index. The eighteenth-century characterisation of Ireland as Róisín Dubh increased the name's popularity and since the poet James Clarence Mangan (1803–49) translated it as 'Dark Rosaleen' that name became popular too.

SEOSAIMHÍN

The Irish version of Josephine, a formation from Joseph, some say by Napoleon Bonaparte's first wife. Josephine grew in popularity with the male name as the cult of St Joseph increased and the Irish form is a diminutive of the Irish Seosamh.

SHEILA (SÍLE)

The name comes from Cecilia, a Roman family name originally meaning 'blind'. The Irish form came first, as an adaptation of the name of the patron saint of music that arrived with the Anglo-Normans. Its great popularity led to its persistent English form and its use as an inoffensive generic term for 'girl' or 'young woman' in Australia.

SIBÉAL

The Irish equivalent of Isobel, which was the
Spanish form of Elizabeth. It was one of many
non-Irish names for which Irish versions were
found to satisfy a fashionable and patriotic
demand at the time of the Gaelic revival. It is
taken also as the Irish form of Sybil, a Greek
word meaning 'wise woman'.

SINEAD (SINÉAD)

The Irish form of Jane which came with the
Anglo-Normans as Jehane, a female form of
John. Its Irish form devised on demand has
survived as a very popular name.

SIOBHAN (SIOBHÁN)

The Irish form of Susan (from the Hebrew
meaning 'lily') or Joan. Like Jane, which became
Sinéad, the name Joan came to Ireland with the
Anglo-Normans and though the two names
have a common origin they produced two distinct
and very popular names in Irish.

SIVE (SADHBH)

The word means 'sweetness' and was the name of the mother of Oisín who spent part of her life as a fawn because of an enchantment by the Dark Druid, a persistent enemy of the Fianna. Another Sadhbh was the daughter of the goddess-queen Maedhbh. The name received a theatrical accolade with J. B. Keane's successful play *Sive* (1959).

SORCHA

The word means 'radiant' and though native Irish has been taken, without authority, as an equivalent of Sarah and by extension Sally. The English name is biblical and means 'queen'.

TREASA

The word means 'strength' and because of its similarity to the French Thérèse was accepted as the Irish version of the name. Its popularity and that of the English name Teresa increased greatly at the canonisation of St Thérèse of Lisieux (1873–97) in 1925.

UNA (ÚNA)

The name is Irish but of uncertain origin. It was sufficiently widespread by the sixteenth century to influence the temporary Doneraile resident Edmund Spenser (?1552–99) to use it for the character representing the true religion in *The Faerie Queene* (1590, 1596), the name suiting the unity of the theme. It is sometimes used as the equivalent of Winifred because of the supposed resemblance between it and Winny.

SELECT BIBLIOGRAPHY

Attwater, Donald. (rev: Catherine Rachel John). *The Penguin Dictionary of Saints*. London, 1985.

Coughlan, Ronan. *Irish Christian Names*. Belfast, 1985.

Cresswell, Julia. *Irish First Names*. Glasgow, 1996.

Berresford Ellis, Peter. *A Dictionary of Irish Mythology*. London, 1987.

Flanagan, Laurence. *Favourite Irish Names for Children*. Dublin, 1993.

McMahon, Sean. *Rekindling the Faith*. Cork & Dublin, 1996.

Ó Corráin, Donnchadh and Fidelma Maguire. *Irish Names*. Dublin, 1990.

Ó Droighneáin, Muiris. *An Sloinnteoir Gaeilge agus An tAinmeoir*. Belfast, 1987.

Sykes, Egerton. (rev: Alan Kendall). *Who's Who in Non-Classical Mythology*. London, 1993.

Woulfe, Patrick. *Irish Names for Children*. Dublin, 1923.